CHANGING THE WORLD
ONE KITCHEN AT A TIME

A SERIES PRESENTED BY
CHILDREN'S CULINARY INSTITUTE

";@&^>*&*@&^!%$@#"
- Mary Mallon

"She fought and struggled and cursed," Officer Baker recalled, "I told the policemen to pick her up and put her in the ambulance. This we did, and the ride down to the hospital was quite a wild one." Officer Baker, whose own father died of typhoid fever, described having to sit on Mallon the entire way to the hospital.

-John Steele Gordon reporter for "American Heritage"

You have been taught the right way to wash your hands at home, at school, and in your cooking classes!

Wet your hands with clean running water, turn off the tap, and apply soap. Lather your hands by rubbing them together with the soap. Lather the backs of your hands as well. Do this for at least 20 seconds. Rinse your hands using a clean towel or air dryer.

The reason we do this is to stop the spread of germs that can cause illness. We do this to keep ourselves and others from getting sick. It is especially important when we are cooking because some germs can be carried through food.

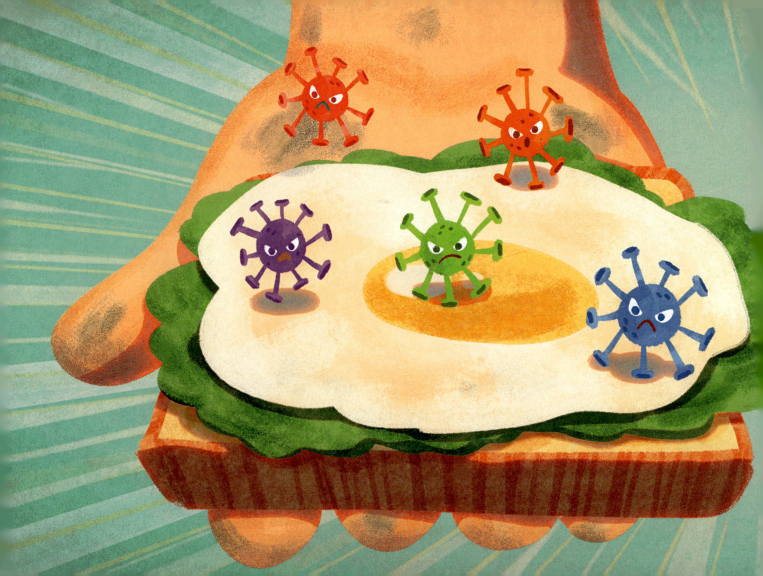

Key times to wash your hands:
Before, during, and after preparing food
Before and after eating food
Before and after caring for someone who is sick

It is hard to imagine a time in history when washing hands was not a normal everyday thing to do. It is true, however, that there was a time when it was not a commonly accepted practice.

Mary Mallon was born in 1869 in Ireland, which was just 17 years after The Great Potato Famine. She was 10 years old when the blight returned and threatened a second famine in Ireland. There were also many battles with the land owners, who were mostly from England and the land workers, who were the Irish locals.

The main source of money and food in Ireland was potato crops. A disease or "blight" that destroyed both the leaves, and the edible roots or tubers of the potato plant for four straight years 1845-1849 caused a famine.
Famine– extreme scarcity of food.

It was not surprising that Mary wanted to leave Ireland to live with her aunt and uncle in New York, in the United States of America, when she was fifteen.

Many immigrants entering the USA believed there were better opportunities there. Those leaving their countries for the Americas hoped for better jobs, and more food. They had to sail on large ships for weeks to get to this land of hope.

Between 1870 and 1900 there were more than 12 million immigrants entering the USA. **Immigrants** are people who move to a new country to live permanently.

Typhoid is a bacterial infection that can spread throughout the body, affecting many organs. Without prompt treatment, it can cause serious complications, and can be fatal. It's caused by a bacterium called salmonella typi, which is related to the bacteria that cause salmonella food poisoning. It can be greatly reduced by using good hygiene.

Good Hygiene is when you keep yourself and your cook area clean.

Mary decided to move from New York City to Manhattan, New York, and start a new job. Shortly after beginning her new job, several members of the new family she was working for, as well as other staff in the house, started having symptoms of typhoid fever. This continued family after family, and city after city for seven years.

One family rented a summer home on Oyster Bay, and hired Mary as a cook. When they got sick, the landlord was worried that no one would rent his house. He had the pipes, faucets, and toilets tested. They all came back negative for typhoid.

An investigator was called into a Park Avenue home to determine the cause of another typhoid outbreak. He recognized the description of an Irish cook who had been at the other homes where typhoid had broken out, and that she would frequently leave without any forwarding address.

An asymptomatic person is a person that has become infected with a pathogen, but does not show signs or symptoms. Although unaffected by the pathogen, carriers can pass it on to others. Scientists calculate that between 1% and 6% of people infected with salmonella typi become **chronic** asymptomatic carriers like Mary. **Chronic**-persisting for a long time or constantly recurring.

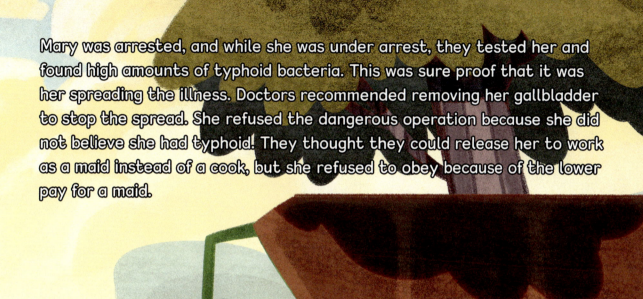

Mary was arrested, and while she was under arrest, they tested her and found high amounts of typhoid bacteria. This was sure proof that it was her spreading the illness. Doctors recommended removing her gallbladder to stop the spread. She refused the dangerous operation because she did not believe she had typhoid! They thought they could release her to work as a maid instead of a cook, but she refused to obey because of the lower pay for a maid.

When Mary was arrested, they took her away in an ambulance. It took five policemen to control her, and one doctor who had to sit on her to keep her in the vehicle.

A maid would earn $20 a month, and a cook could earn $50 a month.

Mary was quarantined on an island just off the coast of New York for three years. She agreed to not work as a cook anymore in exchange for release. She struggled for several years with not making enough money. She decided to use fake names and work as a cook again. Once again, everywhere she worked people got typhoid.

Mary Mallon earned a nick-name that has lasted through history. She is known as "Typhoid Mary"

There were 53 known cases of typhoid fever, and three deaths linked back to Mary. However, officials believe the cases to be much higher than what was recorded.

Bacteria is especially easy to spread to foods that do not get cooked before serving. The heat from cooking helps to kill most bacteria.

It is fun to cook for ourselves and others. We always need to be safe. Get help from adults when we need it, and always wash our hands when we are cooking!

Using soap makes a big difference. Washing your hands with soap and water will remove more germs and bacteria than hand sanitiser or water alone.

Recipe for Irish Stew

2 1/2 pounds lamb shoulder, cut into large chunks

1 1/2 pounds carrots, peeled and cut into 2-inch pieces

3 pounds potato, diced

1 1/2 pounds onion, diced

2 sprigs fresh thyme

4 sprigs fresh parsley

1 bay leaf

5 cups beef stock

1 teaspoon salt

1/2 teaspoon ground black pepper

Directions

1. Add oil to a large heavy pan over medium-high heat.
2. Brown the lamb on all sides, remove and set aside.
3. Add the carrots, potatoes and onions to the pan and cook slightly, coating with the fat and juices from the lamb.
4. Add the lamb back to the pan along with the thyme and parsley.
5. Add the beef stock, salt and pepper. Partially cover with a lid and cook on a low simmer for 2 hours.
6. After 2 hours remove the thyme and parsley sprigs and the bay leaf.

About Children's Culinary Institute

Children's Culinary institute is a program that teaches avid home cooks how to reach out into their communities and to teach children kitchen skills. We operate with our highest goal being the creation of a brighter food future for everyone. We build skills and reinforce the day-to-day school learning through hands on kitchen knowledge and confidence. Our secondary goal is brining sustainability to families with time together, and greater health and sense of being in their communities. To become part of our community, and to teach with our curriculum, reach out to us, and we will help you use your skills to reach out to others.

A Note from the Chef:

I feel bad for poor Mary. She was a carrier of an illness she didn't understand. Even doctors and scentists didn't know a lot about asymptomatic people. I do think we can learn as much from the bad situations as we can from the good ones. We can be grateful for how much we have learned about bacteria and food. While Mary had it rough, we learned a lot from her, and I do admire all the things I read about her being so feisty and standingup for what she thought was right. I will also always be sure my hands are washed! Thank you Mary Mallon- Chef Arlena Strode

Made in the USA
Middletown, DE
26 March 2024